A Tail of a Golden Retriever
by
Lisa Andrews

Storyline:

Meet Bonji: The book opens with Sarah and Mike, a young couple, finally welcoming their dream puppy, Bonji, a golden retriever. Sarah, an avid dog lover, is eager to raise a well-behaved and happy companion. Mike, a first-time dog owner, is apprehensive but excited.

Puppyhood Adventures (Chapters 1-5): The book dives into the adorable chaos of puppyhood. Hilarious anecdotes detail house-training mishaps, teething woes, and the boundless energy of a growing pup. Sarah guides readers through the process of puppy socialization classes, vet visits, and the importance of establishing a positive training routine.

Chapter 1: The Golden Dream Comes True

- Introduces Sarah and Mike, a young couple excited to welcome their new Golden Retriever puppy.
- Details their preparations for the puppy's arrival, like setting up a puppy playpen, buying leash and collar, and puppy-proofing the house.
- We meet Bonji for the first time! Describe his adorable clumsiness and overwhelming cuteness.
- Ends with the initial shock of caring for a puppy - sleepless nights, potty training accidents, and the never-ending chewing.

Setting the Scene:

The chapter opens with a warm and inviting description of Sarah and Mike's home. Hints about their personalities are woven in - perhaps a dog-themed throw pillow, a well-worn copy of a dog training book, or a framed picture of their childhood pets.

Anticipation Builds:

The narrative shifts to Sarah, brimming with excitement. Today's the day! She checks her phone, refreshing the countdown app they set for picking up their puppy. Mike, a touch apprehensive (but secretly excited), tries to act calm, reminding Sarah of the last-minute puppy proofing they need to do.

Welcome Home, Bonji!

The scene shifts to the heart of the chapter - meeting their Golden Retriever puppy. Describe the breeder's kennel, the first glimpse of the fluffy ball of fur, and the instant connection Sarah feels. Mike's initial hesitation melts away as the playful pup steals his heart with a clumsy lick on the hand.

Puppy Love in Action:

The chapter follows Sarah and Mike's first chaotic but joyful hours with their new furry family member. Describe the adorable clumsiness of the puppy exploring their home, the first attempt (and inevitable accident) at potty training, and the hilarious struggle to get the tiny pup to settle down for the night.

The Learning Curve Begins:

As the day winds down, a touch of exhaustion settles in. Sarah, determined to be a great puppy parent, opens the dog training book, highlighting the importance of establishing a routine and setting boundaries. Mike, still enchanted by the puppy's cuteness, playfully suggests they might need to rename their home "Fort Chew Toy."

A Glimpse into the Future:

The chapter ends on a heartwarming note. Sarah cradles the sleeping puppy, whispering promises of a happy life filled with love, adventure, and countless golden memories. A montage of future moments can flash through her mind (playing fetch in the park, snuggles on the couch, a first hike together) hinting at the journey that awaits them.

Chapter 1 Elements:

- **Character Introduction:** Establish Sarah and Mike's personalities and their excitement about getting a puppy.
- **Puppy Arrival:** Describe the joy and chaos of welcoming a Golden Retriever puppy into their home.
- **The Learning Curve:** Briefly introduce the challenges and rewards of puppy parenthood.
- **Emotional Connection:** Highlight the bond forming between the couple and their new furry companion.
- **A Look Ahead:** Foreshadow the adventures and experiences that await them with their Golden Retriever.

This storyline sets the stage for the heartwarming and informative journey of raising a Golden Retriever, leaving the reader eager to learn more about Sarah and Mike's experiences with their adorable pup, Bonji.

Chapter 2: Puppy Playtime (and Mishaps!)

- Dives deeper into the challenges and joys of puppyhood.
- Shares funny anecdotes about house-training mishaps, teaching "leave it" and "come" commands with positive reinforcement.
- Introduces the concept of socialization - taking Bonji to puppy playgroups to meet other dogs and people.
- Highlights the importance of proper play for mental and physical development, with tips on choosing safe chew toys and engaging games.
- Ends with a heartwarming story about Bonji bonding with Sarah and Mike during playtime.

Chapter 2: The Chewing Catastrophe

Bonji, a ball of golden fluff with eyes that could melt glaciers, was officially eight weeks old. The initial puppy-moon glow was starting to wear off for Sarah, replaced by a bone-deep exhaustion that rivaled a marathon runner.

The culprit? Bonji's insatiable chewing habit.

He wasn't malicious, just a curious explorer with a mouth that seemed determined to sample every texture the world offered. One minute, Sarah was enjoying a cup of coffee, the next, a table leg was sporting a new set of teeth marks. Her favorite slippers, once a symbol of cozy nights in, now resembled chewed-up cheese.

The first casualty was a brand-new phone charger. Sarah had watched in horror as Bonji, with the agility of a gymnast, snatched it from the coffee table and retreated under the couch. Moments later, triumphant barks announced the destruction of the cable.

Desperate, Sarah turned to Mike, who, bless his heart, seemed oddly unaffected by the chaos.

"He's just a puppy," Mike chuckled, unfazed by the shredded napkin Bonji proudly presented him.

"Easy for you to say," Sarah grumbled, surveying the carnage. "He's chewing everything in sight!"

Determined to save her sanity (and furniture), Sarah embarked on a crash course in puppy training. Armed with chew toys, treats, and a mountain of patience, she started redirecting Bonji's chewing urges to the appropriate outlets. She'd yelp "Ouch!" when he nipped at her hand, offering a squeaky toy instead. Every time he grabbed an off-limits item, it was a firm "No!" followed by a quick replacement with a chew toy accompanied by enthusiastic praise.

It was a slow process. There were setbacks, like the unfortunate incident with the remote control (RIP, channel surfing). But slowly, a glimmer of hope emerged. Bonji started recognizing the difference between "his" toys and everything else.

One evening, Sarah found herself relaxing on the couch with a (surprisingly intact) book in hand. Bonji, nestled at her feet, happily gnawed on a knotted rope toy. A wave of relief washed over her. This wasn't easy, but with consistency and patience, it seemed she might actually survive puppyhood.

Suddenly, a loud thump startled her. Bonji, tail wagging proudly, sat next to her with a triumphant look on his face. In his mouth? Sarah's favorite throw pillow, sporting a single, perfect chew mark right in the center.

Sarah stared at the scene, then at Bonji's innocent expression. A laugh bubbled up from her chest, morphing into full-blown giggles. Maybe surviving puppyhood wouldn't be easy, but it would definitely be an adventure.

Chapter 3: Sharp Teeth and Teething Troubles

- Focuses on the challenges of puppy teething.
- Explains the physical discomfort puppies experience and the resulting chewing behavior.
- Provides tips on redirecting chewing to appropriate toys, using frozen teething rings, and offering safe chew alternatives.
- Discusses the importance of scheduling regular vet visits for checkups and vaccinations.
- Ends with a heartwarming moment of Bonji learning a new trick (like "sit" or "shake") despite the teething discomfort.

Chapter 3: The Unexpected Teacher

Bonji, no longer the clumsy ball of fluff he once was, bounced with youthful enthusiasm towards the park gates. Sarah, leash in hand, chuckled at his eagerness. Today was their first official group puppy training session. Sarah, a first-time dog owner, was a mix of nervous and excited.

Reaching the designated area, Sarah was greeted by a cacophony of barks and excited whimpers. A motley crew of pups, ranging from fluffy poodles to lumbering Bernese Mountain dogs, explored and sniffed each other with boundless curiosity. Bonji, tail wagging furiously, strained at the leash, eager to join the fun.

A tall woman with a kind smile and a name badge that read "Melanie, Trainer" approached them. Sarah explained her anxieties about puppy training and Bonji's tendency to chew on everything in sight. Melanie offered a warm reassurance, "Don't worry, that's part of the puppy package! We're here to help you both navigate this stage."

The training session began. Melanie expertly guided the group through basic commands like "sit," "stay," and "come." Bonji, initially distracted by the other pups, struggled to focus. Sarah felt a pang of discouragement.

Just then, a tiny, white ball of fluff with a determined glint in its eyes caught Bonji's attention. It was a Shih Tzu puppy named Luna, owned by a young woman named Emily. Luna, despite her size, approached Bonji with an assertive confidence.

Bonji, usually the dominant one, seemed mesmerized. Luna, with perfect obedience, sat in front of him, earning a treat from Emily. As if on cue, Bonji mimicked Luna's pose, his brown eyes pleading for a reward. Sarah, surprised, reached into her treat pouch and praised Bonji.

This unexpected turn of events sparked a change. Throughout the session, whenever Bonji wavered, Luna would appear, a tiny white beacon of focus. With each successful "sit" or "stay" from Luna, Bonji would follow suit, earning a treat and Sarah's happy praise.

By the end of the session, Bonji was a changed pup. He sat patiently, attention directed towards Sarah, a newfound respect sparkling in his eyes. Sarah marveled at how this unlikely friendship had become a catalyst for Bonji's learning.

As they left the park, Sarah thanked Emily. "Honestly," Emily replied, "Luna learned more from Bonji's enthusiasm than the other way around! Seems they needed each other today."

Walking home, Sarah realized that training wouldn't be a solo mission. It would be a journey of learning, not just for Bonji, but for her as well. And sometimes, the best teachers come in the most unexpected packages, with four tiny paws and a determined spirit.

Chapter 4: Adventures in the Park

- Introduces the concept of leash training and taking Bonji on short walks in a safe and controlled environment.
- Shares the joy of exploring the outdoors with your dog, describing the sights, smells, and social interaction with other dog owners at the park.
- Emphasizes the importance of socialization for building confidence and preventing leash reactivity.
- Might include a humorous anecdote about encountering an overly enthusiastic dog at the park and how Sarah handled the situation.
- Ends on a positive note, showcasing the growing bond between Bonji, Sarah, and Mike during their park adventures.

Chapter 4: Chewing Blues and Puppy Playdates

Bonji, a ball of golden fluff with boundless energy, was no stranger to mischief. At 12 weeks old, his world was a whirlwind of exploration, fueled by needle-sharp teeth and an insatiable curiosity. Sarah, still adjusting to life as a puppy parent, was starting to understand the full meaning of the phrase "puppy piranha."

The latest casualty: Sarah's favorite pair of slippers. They weren't completely destroyed, just sporting a new set of jagged holes courtesy of Bonji's gnawing. A sigh escaped her lips as she picked up the mangled remains. This wasn't the first, nor would it be the last, casualty of Bonji's teething phase.

Suddenly, a yelp cut through the air. Bonji, sprawled on the living room rug with a defiant expression, was nursing a sore mouth. Sarah rushed over, concern washing over her. Thankfully, a quick examination revealed no serious damage, just a bruised gum from chewing on something far too hard.

Remembering the advice from the puppy socialization class, Sarah grabbed Bonji's favorite squeaky toy. With a playful shake, she offered it up. Bonji, momentarily forgetting his woes, launched himself at the toy, his tail wagging furiously as he wrestled it with renewed gusto.

Relief washed over Sarah. Positive reinforcement, it seemed, was the key. Just then, her phone buzzed. It was a message from Emily, another puppy owner she met at the class. They had planned a playdate at the park that afternoon. Perfect timing, thought Sarah. Maybe some interaction with another pup would tire Bonji out and keep him out of trouble.

The park was abuzz with activity. Leashed dogs of all shapes and sizes explored the grassy expanse, sniffing and greeting each other with enthusiastic wagging tails. Sarah spotted Emily, a friendly woman with a bouncy Labrador puppy named Luna.

The two puppies, initially hesitant, soon warmed up to each other. They chased each other in playful circles, tumbled in the grass, and explored every nook and cranny of the park with boundless curiosity. Sarah and Emily watched with amusement, sharing stories and advice about their new canine companions.

The playdate was a success. Bonji, exhausted from his romp with Luna, flopped down in the backseat on the way home, his little golden tongue lolling out in a contented sigh. Sarah reached back and scratched behind his ears, a wave of affection washing over her. Despite the chewing woes, the sleepless nights, and the constant stream of drool, there was no denying the immense joy Bonji brought into her life.

As they pulled into the driveway, Sarah noticed a new chew toy – a bright red rubber ring shaped like a bone – lying on the porch. A note attached read, "Welcome to the neighborhood, Bonji! Love, The Johnsons (and Max, the Golden Retriever)." Sarah smiled. Perhaps puppy parenthood wouldn't be quite so solitary after all.

Chapter 5: School Days: Puppy Kindergarten

- Discusses the importance of puppy socialization classes.
- Details the benefits of learning basic obedience commands in a controlled environment with a professional trainer.
- Shares funny or heartwarming moments from puppy class, showcasing Bonji's progress and Sarah's interaction with other dog owners.
- Introduces the concept of clicker training or other positive reinforcement methods for effective training.
- Ends with a sense of accomplishment as Bonji masters a new command learned in puppy class.

The morning sun streamed through the living room window, illuminating a scene of utter destruction. Scattered across the plush carpet were the mangled remains of my favorite slippers. Fluffy stuffing littered the floor like fallen snow, mocking my previous attempts at house training. In the center of the mayhem, tail wagging furiously, sat Bonji, a nine-month-old Golden Retriever with a mischievous glint in his golden eyes.

"Bonji!" I exclaimed, a mixture of exasperation and amusement in my voice. He tilted his head, ears perked, tongue lolling out in a goofy grin. Did he even know what he'd done? Probably not. Golden Retrievers were notorious for their chewing habits at this stage, and my poor slippers were the latest victims.

I sighed, kneeling down to pick up the shredded remains. "Oh, buddy," I said, stroking his soft fur. "You're a menace, you know that?" He responded by nuzzling my hand, his sandpapery tongue leaving a trail of wet kisses. It was hard to stay mad at that adorable face.

Picking up a discarded squeaky toy from the floor, I held it in front of him. "See, Bonji? This is what chew toys are for." He eyed the toy with interest, then back at my hand, holding a defiant shred of slipper. This was it. Time for a training session.

Grabbing a bag of treats from the pantry, I led Bonji outside. The backyard was his personal playground, a sprawling expanse of green perfect for zoomies and fetch. I tossed the squeaky toy across the grass, and he was off like a golden bullet, bounding after it with boundless energy.

As he returned, the toy clutched triumphantly in his jaws, I knelt down and offered a small treat. "Good boy, Bonji!" I praised him, taking the toy gently and tossing it again. This time, he dropped the toy eagerly before me, anticipating another reward. We repeated this routine for a good twenty minutes, the frustration of the chewed slippers fading with each successful retrieve.

Monologue:

"Golden Retrievers," I muttered to myself, wiping sweat from my brow. "They're like furry bundles of sunshine... and chewed furniture. But for all the trouble they cause, wouldn't trade this little monster for the world. He may have a mischievous streak a mile wide, but the love in his eyes and the way he wags his tail for the simplest things… it melts your heart every time."

By the end of the play session, Bonji was panting happily, tongue lolling out in a satisfied grin. As I led him back inside, I noticed he wasn't eyeing the furniture quite as intently. Maybe, just maybe, the training was starting to sink in. Or maybe he was just tired. Either way, I was cautiously optimistic.

Raising a puppy was a constant battle of chewed possessions, spilled water bowls, and muddy paw prints. But with each passing day, Bonji was learning, growing, and becoming more than just a pet. He was becoming a loyal friend, a furry confidante, and a source of endless amusement (and maybe a little frustration). It was a messy, chaotic journey, but one I wouldn't trade for anything. After all, life with a Golden Retriever was never dull.

Growing Up Golden (Chapters 6-12): As Bonji matures, the story tackles common challenges like adolescence, separation anxiety, and basic obedience training. Sarah shares tips on using positive reinforcement techniques, building a strong bond through play and exercise, and navigating potential behavioral issues like chewing or barking.

Chapter 6: The Teenage Terror (or, The Chewing Monster)

- This chapter dives into the often-unruly phase of adolescence.
- Bonji's boundless energy can turn destructive.
- Sarah offers solutions for managing chewing habits, redirecting energy with appropriate toys and chew options, and providing ample exercise to tire him out.
- **Expert Tip:** A veterinarian or trainer can be interviewed to discuss common behavioral issues during adolescence and offer training techniques for curbing destructive chewing.

Chapter 6: The Great Escape Artist

The morning sun streamed through the living room window, casting a warm glow on Sarah curled up on the couch. A soft whimper roused her. Blinking away sleep, she saw Bonji, his golden fur shimmering in the light, standing next to the couch with a sheepish grin. In his mouth, he held the mangled remains of a brand new pair of gardening gloves.

Sarah's Monologue:

Ugh, not again! This is the third pair of gloves this month. Bonji, you furry menace! (Sighs) I know, I know, it's my fault for leaving them within reach. But honestly, how can I resist those puppy-dog eyes? Still, replacing gardening gloves is getting expensive. Maybe it's time to invest in those chew toys shaped like gloves... no, that's just encouraging him!

Scene:

Sarah reached out, pretending to pet Bonji's head. He wagged his tail excitedly, oblivious to the mischief he'd caused. With a playful growl, Sarah snatched the tattered glove, earning a playful nip on her hand.

"Alright, alright," she chuckled, surrendering the other glove. "Let's head outside, Mr. Destroyer of Gloves, and see if we can find some activities that don't involve ruining my gardening supplies."

She grabbed her favorite red leash and clipped it onto Bonji's collar. He bounded towards the door, his tail a blur of golden fur. Sarah followed him out into the cool morning air.

Action:

They headed straight for the park across the street. Bonji strained at the leash, eager to greet his canine buddies. Sarah let him off the leash once they reached the designated dog area. He sprinted towards a group of playful retrievers, barking with joy.

Sarah's Monologue:

Watching him run like that, it's hard to believe he was ever that tiny, clumsy ball of fluff. Remember that first day, Bonji? You were barely bigger than my hand and tripped over your own paws. Now you're a whirlwind of golden fur and boundless energy.

Sarah found a shady spot on a bench and pulled out a book. She watched Bonji weave through the pack of dogs, chasing frisbees and initiating playful wrestling matches.

A New Challenge:

Suddenly, a loud chirp caught Bonji's attention. A small squirrel darted across the grass, its bushy tail a twitching red flag. Bonji locked eyes with the squirrel, his playful mood replaced by a determined glint. Before Sarah could react, he took off in a blur, his leash trailing behind him.

Sarah's Monologue:

Oh no, Bonji! Don't even think about it! Squirrels are your kryptonite. (Jumps up) Come back, Bonji! Come back here right now!

The Chase:

Sarah scrambled to her feet and sprinted after Bonji. The leash, dragging behind him, snagged on a tree root, tripping him momentarily. Sarah used the opportunity to grab the leash and yank him back.

"Bonji! No squirrels! Remember what we talked about?"

Bonji whined and pawed at the leash, his eyes fixed on the squirrel now perched on a low branch, taunting him.

Sarah's Monologue:

(Sighs) It's a losing battle, isn't it? You're as stubborn as your golden retriever namesake. Okay, here's the plan. We'll head back home, and I'll dig out that old stuffed squirrel toy you haven't touched in months. Maybe that will do the trick.

She turned and started walking toward the park exit, Bonji reluctantly trailing behind her.

A Lesson Learned:

As they walked, Sarah couldn't help but smile. Even with all the chewed gloves and squirrel-chasing escapades, she wouldn't trade Bonji for the world. He brought a level of joy and excitement into her life that she never knew existed.

Sarah's Monologue:

You may be a mischievous furball, Bonji, but you're my mischievous furball. And I wouldn't have it any other way. Just maybe, next time, I'll leave the gloves out of sight. After all, a little challenge never hurt anyone, right?

Chapter Ends:

Sarah and Bonji continued their walk home, their bond strengthened by the morning's adventure. Bonji might have been a handful, but their love and understanding for each other continued to grow.

Chapter 7: Separation Anxiety Blues

- Bonji might struggle with being left alone.
- The chapter explores the causes and signs of separation anxiety in dogs.
- Sarah details methods for gradually increasing alone time, providing comfort items, and creating a positive association with departure.
- **Expert Tip:** A certified animal behaviorist could offer additional strategies for managing separation anxiety.

Chapter 7: The Big Splash (with Golden Monologue)

The summer sun beat down on Central Park, turning the asphalt paths into shimmering mirages. Sarah, beads of sweat clinging to her forehead, clutched the leash nervously. Bonji, her exuberant golden retriever, bounced at her side, his tail a metronome of pure joy. Today was the day they were tackling the dreaded doggy pool.

Memories of her childhood dog, a skittish Yorkie terrified of water, swirled in Sarah's mind. "What if Bonji hates it?" she fretted.

Bonji, oblivious to her worries, pulled at the leash, his golden fur shimmering in the sunlight. They reached the designated dog park, a haven of four-legged fun. A chorus of barks filled the air as Sarah scanned the area. There, nestled amidst happy pups chasing frisbees, stood the infamous doggy pool. It wasn't massive, but for a dog who'd only ever seen water from a drinking bowl, it might as well have been an ocean.

Taking a deep breath, Sarah approached the pool. As she lowered the leash, Bonji, sensing her hesitation, whined. Sarah knelt, rubbing his head. "It's okay, buddy," she reassured him, her voice barely a whisper.

Bonji's Monologue:

(Whining softly)

"This is weird, Sarah. This thing smells funny, and it's all blue. Plus, there's this weird squeaking noise coming from those things bobbing around. Are those…dolphins? Are we at the beach? Where's the sand? This leash is really cutting into my neck, can you loosen it up a bit?"

Sarah chuckled at the image of Bonji picturing the pool as an ocean adventure. "Those are squeaky toys, silly boy," she explained, picking up a bright yellow duck. "See? Fun things!"

Bonji eyed the duck warily. It looked suspiciously like the squeaky things Sarah used to torture him with at bath time. He let out a skeptical snort.

Suddenly, a blur of brown fur shot past them. A chocolate Labrador, tongue lolling out, launched itself into the pool with an almighty splash. The water erupted in a spray of droplets. Bonji, caught off guard, yelped and took a startled step back.

Sarah knelt again, holding the duck near the edge of the pool. "See how much fun that dog is having? Maybe you just need a taste."

Hesitantly, Bonji inched forward. He dipped his long pink tongue into the cool water, the taste foreign but not unpleasant. Curiosity piqued, he took another tentative step forward. The water lapped at his paws, making him shiver slightly.

(Thinking)

"Hmmm, wet. Not bad, actually. Maybe a little swim wouldn't hurt…"

Just then, a playful bark echoed behind him. A bouncy terrier mix, all elbows and enthusiasm, bounced into him, sending Bonji tumbling headfirst into the pool.

A moment of stunned silence followed. Then, an eruption of joyous barking filled the air. Bonji, sputtering and surprised, found himself paddling furiously, his legs churning the water. The world became a symphony of splashing and yapping. He chased the bright yellow duck, snapping at it playfully. The cool water was exhilarating, a refreshing escape from the summer heat.

Sarah watched in delight as Bonji transformed into a water-loving maniac. He chased after other dogs, frolicked with the squeaky toys, and even attempted a (somewhat comical) doggy paddle.

(Smiling)

"That's my boy! You're a natural!"

Bonji, dripping wet and sporting a manic grin, shook himself off, showering Sarah with a spray of cool water. He barked playfully, his tail a blur of excited wagging.

(Thinking)

"Wow, this water stuff is actually pretty awesome! Who knew? Maybe next time, I'll even try that diving thing the Lab was doing. Now, who's up for fetch?"

As the sun began to dip below the horizon, Sarah and Bonji left the park, both exhausted but exhilarated. Bonji, tongue lolling out in contentment, curled up at Sarah's feet in the car ride home. Today, he had discovered a new joy, a love for the cool embrace of water. And Sarah, watching him sleep, realized that sometimes, the biggest adventures started with a single hesitant step.

Chapter 8: Obedience Boot Camp (or, Sit, Stay, and Come... Eventually!)

- This chapter delves into the importance of consistent obedience training during adolescence.
- Sarah details basic commands like sit, stay, come, and heel, using positive reinforcement methods with clear instructions, treats, and praise.
- The chapter acknowledges the challenges of a strong-willed adolescent but emphasizes patience and consistency.

Chapter 8: The Big Splash

The summer sun beat down on Maple Street, turning the asphalt into a shimmering mirage. Inside the Miller house, Sarah desperately tried to stay cool, fanning herself with a magazine as Bonji, her golden retriever, whined at her feet.

"It's too hot to play fetch, buddy," Sarah sighed, scratching him behind the ears. "Maybe later, when the sun goes down a bit."

Bonji whined again, his tail thumping a restless rhythm against the hardwood floor. Sarah understood his frustration. Golden Retrievers, especially young ones like Bonji, were built for action. This relentless heat was torture for his energetic spirit.

Just then, an idea struck Sarah. She grabbed a worn blue beach ball from the corner and bounced it in front of Bonji. His head shot up, ears perked, and his tail went into overdrive.

"Beach ball?" Sarah asked, her voice rising with a playful lilt.

Bonji let out a bark that could only be described as ecstatic. This was a game he understood. Sarah grabbed her keys and a leash, a mischievous grin spreading across her face.

"Alright, boy," she said, clipping the leash on. "Let's go find some water."

At the Park

The town park was a haven on a scorching day. Lush trees provided shade, and the faint trickle of a man-made stream offered a tantalizing promise of coolness. Sarah found a quiet spot under a large willow and unclipped Bonji's leash. He bounded ahead, sniffing every interesting blade of grass and discarded toy.

Sarah reached the stream, a meandering waterway that was just a few inches deep at most. It was perfect.

She knelt by the water's edge, bouncing the beach ball. "Go get it, Bonji!" she called out.

He didn't need telling twice. With a joyful bark, Bonji bolted towards the water, his golden fur catching the sunlight. He reached the stream, skidded to a halt, and plunged his entire head in, sending a spray of water flying.

Sarah laughed, a joyful sound echoing through the park. Bonji emerged, shaking his head like a furry dog at a car wash, the bright blue ball clutched triumphantly in his teeth.

Bonji's Monologue (Internal)

(Water dripping from my fur, I trot back to Sarah, tail wagging a mile a minute. This is the best day ever! The heat doesn't bother me as much when there's water involved. And that ball? It's the perfect size for carrying, splashing with, and maybe even giving a good chomp or two. Sarah throws it again, and I know the routine. Run, splash, grab, repeat! Man, I love being a dog.)

Sarah threw the ball again and again. Bonji chased it with tireless enthusiasm, his golden body a blur against the green backdrop. Each time he emerged from the water, he looked happier, his tongue lolling out in a blissful doggy grin.

Back Home

As the sun began its descent, casting long shadows across the park, Sarah decided it was time to head home. Bonji, tired but content, lumbered beside her, the beach ball bobbing in his mouth like a soggy trophy.

Back in the cool confines of the house, Sarah collapsed onto the couch, a cold glass of lemonade in hand. Bonji, dripping wet and panting, dropped the now-deflated beach ball at her feet.

"Good boy," Sarah said, patting his head. "You earned a nice long nap after all that playing."

Bonji nestled beside her, his wet fur leaving a damp patch on the cushion. Sarah didn't mind. He was the best dog a girl could ask for, and all he craved was a little love, a little play, and maybe just a splash of water on a hot summer day.

Chapter 9: Leash Manners: From Pulling to Polite

- Walks can be a battleground with an untrained pup.
- Sarah provides strategies for leash training, teaching Bonji loose leash walking, using a gentle leader or front-clip harness if needed, and incorporating positive reinforcement during walks.

Chapter 9: The Unexpected

The crisp autumn air nipped at my fur as I bounded alongside Sarah. Leaves, ablaze in gold and crimson, crunched under our paws as we explored the winding paths of our favorite park. Life as a Golden Retriever was pretty darn good. Waking up to Sarah's sleepy smile, chasing squirrels in the backyard, and evening snuggles on the couch - it was a routine I wouldn't trade for all the belly rubs in the world.

Suddenly, Sarah stopped, a frown creasing her brow. My tail thumped the ground, confused. This wasn't like her. Walks were supposed to be all about playful energy, not furrowed foreheads.

"Bonji," she sighed, pulling out her phone, "I have some news..."

My ears perked up. News? Was it treat day already? Maybe a trip to the dog park filled with new friends to sniff?

Sarah sat on a park bench, patting the spot beside her. I nestled in, my head on her lap.

(Sarah's Monologue):

"Bonji, you know how much I love spending time with you, right? You're the best dog a girl could ask for. But lately, things have been… different."

(She sighed, stroking my fur absentmindedly.)

"Remember how we talked about getting married someday? Well, Mike and I… we decided to take the leap! We're getting married!"

My tail thumped excitedly. Wedding? Did that mean cake? Extra belly rubs during the celebration?

(Sarah's Monologue continues):

"It's going to be amazing, Bonji. But…" her voice trailed off. "There's just one little thing. We want to start a family… you know, with babies."

A baby? A tiny human to play fetch with? This sounded like the best news ever! I wagged my tail so hard my whole body wiggled.

(Sarah's Monologue continues, a hint of worry creeping in):

"I know you love playing, Bonji. But babies are delicate. We need to make sure you're gentle and well-behaved around them. There will be a lot of changes, and I need to know you're up for it."

A hesitant lick to her hand, my tail still wagging. Of course, I'd be gentle! Babies were just smaller versions of humans to love, right?

(Sarah's Monologue softens):

"Oh, Bonji, you're going to be the best big brother ever. I know it. We'll just have to learn this new adventure together. You, me, and our little family."

A warmth spread through me. Family. It seemed like a bigger, more exciting pack. And as long as Sarah was by my side, I was ready for whatever adventure awaited us.

Chapter 10: Social Butterfly or Nervous Nelly?

- Golden Retrievers are typically social, but some might be shy.
- The chapter explores dog park etiquette, socialization techniques for shy dogs, and the importance of positive interactions with other dogs for well-being.
- **Expert Tip:** A dog trainer could offer guidance on socialization for shy dogs, recommending classes or appropriate playdates.

Chapter 10: The Big Test

The crisp morning air swirled with nervous energy. Sarah clipped Bonji's leash, the familiar jingle a comforting sound against the pre-dawn quiet. Today was the day – the day of his Canine Good Citizen (CGC) test.

Over the past few months, Sarah had diligently trained Bonji. They'd practiced walking politely on a leash, ignoring distractions, and patiently waiting for commands. Bonji, with his boundless enthusiasm, had tested Sarah's patience at times. But their bond had grown stronger, built on trust and shared treats.

As they approached the park, the testing ground, Bonji's tail thumped a happy rhythm against Sarah's leg. She knelt and scratched behind his ears.

Sarah's Monologue:

"Alright, buddy," she whispered, her voice trembling slightly. "We've come a long way, haven't we? Remember, stay calm, listen good, and most importantly, have fun. I know you can do this."

Bonji stared at her with his soulful brown eyes, his tongue lolling out in a goofy grin. Whether he understood her words or not, he sensed her nervousness. He nudged her hand with his wet nose, a silent reassurance. Sarah chuckled, her anxiety easing.

The testing area bustled with activity. Excited dogs strained at leashes, their owners offering calming words and encouraging pats. Sarah found a spot on the sidelines, observing other dogs navigate the test.

One by one, the dogs were called. They had to walk politely around cones, sit calmly amidst distractions, and allow a stranger to examine them without flinching. Sarah watched, her heart beating a frantic rhythm with each successful passing grade.

Finally, their turn arrived. The calm and collected voice of the evaluator instructed them to begin. Taking a deep breath, Sarah held Bonji's leash firmly but gently.

He surprised her with his focus. He walked with a practiced heel beside her, ignoring the playful barks and yips of the other dogs. He sat patiently as a noisy toy car was rolled past, his eyes fixed on Sarah. When a stranger approached, he allowed them to pet his head and check his ears without a whimper.

Each completed task brought a surge of relief and pride to Sarah. Bonji, the once rambunctious puppy, had transformed into a well-mannered canine citizen.

The evaluator smiled warmly.

"Excellent work! Your dog demonstrated impressive obedience and a calm temperament. He's a true asset to you."

Tears welled up in Sarah's eyes. They had done it! Bonji, with his boundless energy and playful spirit, had aced the test. As the evaluator presented her with the CGC certificate, a wave of emotion washed over her. It was more than just a test; it was a testament to their bond, to the countless hours spent training and playing, and to the unwavering love between a girl and her golden retriever.

Chapter 11: The Great Outdoors: Hiking with your Golden

- Golden Retrievers are active dogs who thrive on exercise.
- This chapter explores the joys and challenges of hiking with a dog.
- Sarah provides tips on choosing dog-friendly trails, conditioning your dog for longer hikes, proper equipment like leashes and poop bags, and being a responsible trail user with your furry companion.

Chapter 11: The Test

The late afternoon sun cast long shadows across the park, dappling the grass where Sarah and Bonji practiced their obedience routine. Bonji, a golden retriever with fur the color of ripe wheat, sat patiently, his tongue lolling out in a goofy grin. He loved these training sessions, not just for the tasty treats that followed, but for the chance to focus solely on Sarah.

"Alright, Bonji," Sarah said, her voice firm but gentle, "one last time. Stay."

She took a few steps back, her heart pounding a little faster than usual. Today was the day for Bonji's "off-leash" test at the park. It was a requirement for him to be officially certified as a therapy dog, a title they had both been working towards for months.

Bonji watched her intently, his tail thumping a steady rhythm against the grass. Sarah took a deep breath and gave the release command, "Go play!"

Bonji bolted forward, a blur of golden fur as he chased a frisbee thrown by another dog owner. Sarah's stomach tightened. The park was bustling with activity – kids playing, dogs barking, squirrels darting across the path. It was a sensory overload for any dog, let alone a playful pup like Bonji.

Minutes stretched into what felt like hours. Sarah watched, a lump forming in her throat, as Bonji weaved through the chaos. He barked excitedly at a group of children playing tag, sniffed curiously at a discarded hot dog wrapper, and even attempted to join a game of fetch with a Labrador twice his size.

Just when Sarah was about to call him back, a young boy, no older than five, tripped and fell onto the pavement, scraping his knee. Tears welled up in his eyes, a loud wail about to erupt. But then, Bonji appeared.

He stopped in front of the boy, his playful energy replaced by a quiet focus. He lowered his head, avoiding eye contact, and nudged the boy's hand with his wet nose. The boy hiccupped, his tears momentarily forgotten. He tentatively reached out and stroked Bonji's soft fur.

Bonji (internal monologue): Woah, what happened here? This little guy looks sad. Maybe he needs a friend? Momma told me to be gentle with kids, so I gotta be careful. (Sniffs the boy's hand) Hmm, smells like… cookies? No time for snacks now, gotta make him feel better.

A small smile crept onto the boy's face. He wrapped his arms around Bonji's neck, burying his face in the fur. The boy's mother rushed over, apologizing profusely and thanking Sarah. Bonji sat patiently, a golden ambassador of comfort, as the woman cleaned her son's scraped knee.

Sarah watched the scene unfold, a wave of relief washing over her. This wasn't what they had practiced, but it was everything Bonji was meant to be – a gentle soul who offered comfort and companionship in moments of need.

Sarah (to Bonji): (Bending down, her voice choked with emotion) Good boy, Bonji. You're the best boy.

Bonji looked up at her, his tail wagging a slow, proud beat.

The off-leash test might not have gone according to plan, but in that moment, Sarah knew they had achieved something far greater. Bonji wasn't just a well-trained dog; he was a furry therapist in the making, a beacon of golden sunshine with a heart full of love.

Chapter 12: Saying "No" with Love (Setting Boundaries for a Happy Dog)

- Setting boundaries and expectations is key to a well-behaved dog.
- Sarah discusses the importance of consistent rules, positive reinforcement for desired behaviors, and gentle but firm correction for unwanted behaviors.
- The chapter emphasizes the importance of positive reinforcement and avoiding harsh punishment.

Chapter 12: The Test

The midday sun beat down on the park, turning the asphalt path into a shimmering mirage. Sarah wiped sweat from her brow, her gaze fixed on Bonji, who bounded ahead, a blur of golden fur chasing a rogue butterfly.

Twelve months. It had been a year since Sarah had brought Bonji home, a tiny ball of fluff with boundless energy and a perpetual chewing obsession. Today, at the park obedience class, was the test day - the culmination of months of "sit," "stay," and "heel" drills.

Bonji, oblivious to the impending test, returned, tail wagging furiously, a triumphant glint in his eyes. He plopped the mangled remains of the butterfly at Sarah's feet, earning a chuckle and a quick scratch behind the ears.

"Alright, Bonji," Sarah said, her voice firm but gentle. "Let's go show Mr. Evans what we've learned."

Mr. Evans, a retired dog trainer with a booming voice and a twinkle in his eye, stood at the other end of the makeshift training ring. A row of hopeful owners and their canine companions awaited their turn.

Anxiety gnawed at Sarah's stomach. Bonji had been a star student throughout the classes, eager to please and quick to learn. But what if the unfamiliar setting, the crowd of dogs, rattled him? What if all their hard work unraveled in a flurry of barks and leash-pulling?

As they stepped into the ring, Sarah took a deep breath. "Bonji, heel," she commanded, her voice steady.

Bonji, sensing her nervousness, nudged her hand with his wet nose. It was a silent reassurance, a promise to try his best. Sarah smiled, the tension easing a little.

Mr. Evans put them through their paces. Sit. Stay. Come. Heel. Each command was a shared breath, a silent communication between Sarah and Bonji. Bonji, fueled by praise and the occasional dog treat, performed flawlessly. He even managed to ignore the playful yelps of a nearby puppy, a feat that usually sent him into a frenzy.

Finally, the test was over. Sarah, her heart overflowing with pride, watched as Mr. Evans approached.

"Well done, Sarah," Mr. Evans boomed, his voice filled with genuine warmth. "And Bonji, you were a champ! You've both come such a long way."

He handed Sarah a certificate, a tangible validation of their success. Bonji, sensing her joy, let out a happy bark and jumped up, showering her face with slobbery kisses.

Later, as they walked home, a tired but happy Bonji trotting by her side, Sarah realized it wasn't just Bonji who had passed the test. She, too, had learned valuable lessons. Patience, consistency, and most importantly, the power of love and understanding.

Bonji's Monologue (Internal)

(Sniffing the air, tail thumping softly)

So many smells! This park is the best. Squirrels hiding in trees, pigeons cooing on the benches… and butterflies! That one was a real challenge, but I caught it! See, Sarah? I'm a good boy. I listened when you told me to "heel," even when Mr. Evans called all the other dogs. Treats help, though. Those little liver things are the best!

Mr. Evans seemed happy with me. He said I was a champ! I wonder what that means? Does it mean I get more butterflies to chase? (Yawns) Maybe later. This obedience stuff is tiring, but I like seeing Sarah smile. Makes my tail wag even harder. She's the best, you know? Always there with a treat and a scratch behind the ears. We're a team, me and Sarah. A good team.

Golden Years (Chapters 13-18):

The book progresses into Bonji's golden years. Sarah delves into the joys of having a well-trained adult dog by your side. They embark on adventures - dog park visits, hikes, and even dog-friendly vacations. The story emphasizes the importance of keeping senior dogs active and engaged, with modifications for their age.

Chapter 13: The Wisdom of Age

- This chapter marks the transition into Bonji's senior years. Sarah reflects on his changing needs and how their routines adapt.
- We see the benefits of consistent training – Bonji calmly navigates walks, responds to commands, and enjoys playtime without the boundless puppy energy.
- A visit to the vet focuses on preventative care for senior dogs, including dental hygiene, joint health, and regular checkups.

Chapter 13: The Patience of Gold

The morning sun streamed through the kitchen window, painting golden squares on the worn wooden floor. Sarah stretched, the familiar creak of her back a stark contrast to the silent slumber of Bonji sprawled beside her. He wasn't a puppy anymore, but at eight years old, his playful spirit hadn't dimmed much.

Except for today.

He hadn't greeted her with his usual enthusiastic tail wags, and his breakfast remained untouched in his bowl. Sarah knelt beside him, concern etching lines on her forehead. "Bonji? Boy, what's wrong?"

He lifted his head, his normally bright eyes dull. A low whine escaped his throat, and he gingerly put weight on his front leg. Sarah's heart lurched.

"Oh, Bonji," she murmured, gently running her fingers along his back.

Bonji's Monologue (Internal)

The walk yesterday wasn't the same. Every step felt heavy, a dull ache throbbing in my leg. The squirrels, those pesky taunts, barely got a flicker of my attention. I wanted to chase, to bark, to be the playful Golden I always am. But the pain held me back.

Sarah, my Sarah, her brow furrowed. I hate to worry her. She's always there, with her gentle touch and her endless supply of belly rubs. She throws the best sticks, even if I can't quite catch them all anymore.

She always knows.

End Monologue

The vet's office was a whirlwind of unfamiliar smells and cold metal surfaces. Sarah held my leash tightly, her reassuring presence a balm in the sterile environment. The vet, a kind woman with gentle hands, examined my leg. Her words were a jumble, but I felt Sarah tense beside me. Arthritis. An old dog problem.

"It won't be a walk in the park," the vet said, her voice soft, "but with medication and some adjustments, we can keep him comfortable."

Comfortable. That was a funny word. My favorite things – chasing squirrels, long walks in the park, fetch in the backyard – all seemed distant now.

Back in the car, Sarah's hand rested on my head

"We'll get through this together, boy," she whispered, her voice thick with emotion.

A warmth bloomed in my chest, a familiar feeling I couldn't quite name. It wasn't the joy of a new squeaky toy, or the thrill of the open field. It was something deeper, a quiet understanding.

Bonji's Monologue (Internal)

Maybe the walks will be shorter, the games less energetic. But Sarah's love, that will never change. And as long as I have her by my side, every day will be a golden adventure, even with a slower step.

End Monologue

Sarah pulled into the driveway, and I nudged my nose against her hand. The familiar scent of home filled my senses. My leg might ache, but with Sarah beside me, every sunrise promised a new adventure, a slower pace, but a love as boundless as ever.

Chapter 14: Adventures Await (Modified)

- This chapter highlights the joys of having a well-trained adult Golden Retriever.
- Sarah and Mike plan activities suitable for Bonji's age, like scenic hikes with plenty of rest breaks, dog park visits during calmer hours, or even dog-friendly kayaking adventures with a life vest for Bonji.
- The emphasis is on keeping him active and engaged in a way that respects his physical limitations.

Chapter 14: The Test

The park was a symphony of scents for Bonji. Pigeons cooed a high note, squirrels chattered a frantic melody, and the underlying bass was the earthy musk of damp grass and well-trodden dirt. He strained at his leash, golden fur shimmering under the morning sun, as Sarah navigated the bustling crowd. Today was the day for his off-leash certification test.

"Easy, boy," Sarah soothed, her voice a familiar counterpoint to the park's cacophony. Bonji whined, his tail thumping a nervous rhythm against her leg. He loved the park, the freedom to chase after frisbees and tumble with other dogs. But the thought of earning Sarah's praise without the reassuring tug of the leash sent shivers down his spine.

They reached the designated training area. Other hopeful pups, a yappy Chihuahua and a sleek Doberman Pinscher, bounced around their handlers. Sarah knelt down, her touch calming Bonji's racing heart.

(Bonji's Monologue)

"This is it, boy," I thought, my ears twitching at the unfamiliar sounds. "Remember everything Sarah taught us. Sit. Stay. Come. Those are the magic words that make her tail wag and her voice go all happy-squeaky."

The trainer, a tall woman with a booming voice, began the test. The Chihuahua, a tiny ball of fluff, bolted at the first command, leaving its owner scrambling. Bonji watched with amusement, a rumble escaping his throat.

"Next up, Bonji and Sarah," the trainer called. Sarah clipped the leash off and stood tall, her eyes meeting his. A silent promise passed between them.

(End Monologue)

Sarah gave him the "sit" command. Bonji obeyed instantly, his body alert but focused. One by one, he aced the commands. "Stay" turned into a statue pose even with a playful butterfly fluttering by. When Sarah called him, he rocketed towards her, a blur of golden fur, his joy echoing in his excited barks.

The trainer beamed. "Congratulations, Bonji and Sarah! You passed with flying colors."

Sarah scooped him up in a hug, burying her face in his fur. "Good boy, Bonji! You did fantastic!" Her voice was thick with emotion.

Bonji wagged his tail so hard his whole body wiggled. He didn't fully understand the test, the leash, or the certification. But he understood the feeling of making Sarah happy, of exceeding her expectations. And that, in his dog world, was the greatest reward of all.

Chapter 15: Golden Games

- This chapter delves into keeping senior Goldens mentally stimulated.
- Sarah introduces games and activities specifically designed for older dogs, like puzzle feeders, scent work games (hiding treats for Bonji to find), or even basic obedience drills with reduced repetition.
- This section could feature interviews with dog trainers specializing in senior dog enrichment.

Chapter 15: The Park Panic

The morning sun cast long shadows across the park as Sarah clipped Bonji's leash. Today was their usual Saturday routine: a brisk walk followed by a free-for-all in the dog park. Bonji, a golden retriever with fur the color of spun sunshine, vibrated with excitement. His tail thumped a happy rhythm against the floor as he danced around Sarah, tongue lolling out in a goofy grin.

"Alright, boy," Sarah chuckled, attaching the leash. "Let's go burn some energy."

The walk to the park was filled with the familiar sights and sounds. Squirrels scampered up oak trees, birds chirped from hidden perches, and the crisp air carried the scent of freshly cut grass. Bonji, ever the explorer, sniffed every lamppost and lampshade with the enthusiasm of a dog sniffing out buried treasure.

Reaching the park entrance, Sarah unclipped the leash. Bonji shot forward like a furry golden missile, a joyous bark erupting from his throat. He weaved between his canine companions, greeting each one with an exuberant wag and a playful shower of slobbery kisses.

Sarah watched with a smile. Watching Bonji interact with other dogs filled her with a warmth that spread through her chest. He was a social butterfly, always eager to make new friends.

Just then, a commotion erupted near the center of the park. A large, unfamiliar dog, all black muscle and sharp teeth, bounded towards a group of smaller dogs, barking ferociously. The smaller dogs scattered, yelping in fear. Bonji, oblivious to the potential danger, trotted up to the new dog with his usual wagging tail.

Sarah's heart lurched. Panic flooded her veins. Her happy-go-lucky Bonji was about to waltz right into a potential brawl.

"Bonji, No!" she screamed, her voice a panicked shriek that cut through the park's cacophony.

Sarah's Monologue:

My legs felt like lead as I sprinted across the park. Every fiber of my being screamed at me to get to Bonji before something terrible happened. My mind raced with terrifying possibilities. What if the big dog attacked? What if Bonji, in his boundless enthusiasm, didn't realize the danger he was in?

The distance between me and Bonji seemed to stretch into an eternity. A primal fear, a mix of love and terror, choked my throat. I wouldn't be able to live with myself if anything happened to him.

(End of Monologue)

Ignoring the curious gazes of other dog owners, Sarah continued her desperate sprint. Each bark, each growl, scraped against her eardrums like nails on a chalkboard. Would she reach him in time?

Chapter 16: The Golden Community

- Broadening the perspective, Sarah interviews other Golden Retriever owners with senior dogs.
- We hear stories about Goldens excelling as therapy dogs in hospitals, visiting patients and offering comfort.
- Another owner might share their experience with a Golden Retriever as a certified service animal, assisting someone with a disability.
- The focus is on the versatility and unwavering loyalty of the breed throughout their lives.

Chapter 16: The Big Splash

The morning sun streamed through the kitchen window, painting golden stripes across the floor. I, Bonji, a golden retriever with fur as bright as sunshine, stretched luxuriously on my bed. A yawn escaped my muzzle, revealing a pink tongue and a row of pearly whites. Today was a special day, a day I'd been dreaming of ever since I learned the glorious concept of water.

"Sarah?" I whined, nudging her hand with my wet nose. "Up! Up! It's adventure time!"

Sarah, my human, stirred with a sleepy groan. "Bonji, not yet," she mumbled, burrowing deeper under the covers.

I wasn't having any of that. Today was the day for our first trip to the lake! Sarah had promised weeks ago, ever since I'd chased the sprinklers in the backyard with unbridled enthusiasm.

"Come on, Sarah!" I barked, a demand disguised as a playful nudge. "The lake beckons!" (Well, not literally, of course. Dogs don't talk. But a retriever can dream, right?)

Finally, Sarah surrendered. With a sleep-tousled head and a smile, she scratched my ears. "Alright, alright, Mr. Eager. Let's get you some water."

The car ride felt like an eternity. Every passing car, every rustle of leaves, fueled my excitement. When the car finally stopped, I nearly burst through the window.

There it was, the lake - a vast expanse of shimmering blue reflecting the morning sky. The air vibrated with the sounds of birdsong and the distant laughter of children. My tail thumped against the backseat like a metronome set to "happy."

Sarah opened the door and I launched myself out, a blur of golden fur and boundless energy. The cool grass tickled my paws as I raced towards the water. Its edge shimmered, beckoning me closer.

"Wait, Bonji!" Sarah called out, but I was already in.

Oh, the glorious sensation! Cool water lapped against my belly, sending shivers of delight down my spine. I splashed and paddled, barking with joy. The world seemed to shrink to this moment - the coolness on my fur, the spray in my face, the sheer, unadulterated joy of being a dog in water.

Suddenly, the ground disappeared beneath my paws. Panic surged through me. I was paddling furiously, but the water seemed to stretch endlessly beneath me.

My head broke the surface, gasping for air. A wave of fear washed over me. I thrashed, desperately trying to find solid ground.

"Bonji!" Sarah's voice, frantic with worry, cut through the panic. I saw her wading in, her face etched with concern.

"Easy, boy," she soothed, her voice calming me down. "Let me help you."

With a gentle hand on my collar, she guided me back to shore. My legs wobbled as I stood on solid ground, the world spinning slightly. I licked her hand gratefully, my heart still pounding.

"You okay, buddy?" she asked, her voice a mixture of relief and scolding.

I whined apologetically, tail tucked between my legs. My grand adventure had gotten a little out of paw.

Sarah chuckled, running a hand through my fur. "Don't worry, pup," she said. "We'll stick to the shallows today. But next time," she winked, "maybe we can try that fancy doggy paddle you were practicing."

Relief washed over me. Next time? There would be a next time! Maybe not a deep-sea exploration, but more water, more fun, more adventures with my human.

And as I settled down by the shore, panting happily with a giant stick in my mouth, I knew one thing for sure: life with Sarah was always going to be one big, wet, tail-wagging adventure.

Chapter 17: A Golden's Love Story (Optional)

- This chapter (optional, depending on the book's length) could be a heartwarming story about a senior Golden Retriever who forms a special bond with someone unexpected.
- Perhaps, it's a lonely neighbor Bonji visits regularly, bringing smiles and companionship.
- This chapter showcases the emotional connection these dogs can offer throughout their lives.

Chapter 17: The Obedience Gamble

The park bustled with activity. Children shrieked, squirrels darted, and frisbees soared through the air. Bonji, my golden retriever pup, a blur of golden fur and boundless energy, strained at the leash. His tail thumped a frantic rhythm against my leg, a constant metronome of excitement.

"Just a few minutes more, buddy," I soothed, kneeling beside him. "We need to practice some focus before playtime."

Bonji whined, tongue lolling out in a goofy grin. At five months old, he was a charming hurricane, a loveable ball of fluff that understood the concept of "sit" about as well as astrophysics.

"Alright, Bonji," I said, taking a deep breath. "Let's try this again. Sit. Stay." I held a treat in front of his nose, then slowly raised it towards the sky.

He watched the treat rise, his head tilting comically. Then, with a dramatic sigh, he plopped onto his haunches.

"Yes!" I exclaimed, clicking my tongue and rewarding him with the treat. His tail wagged furiously, golden fur rippling.

"See, Champ?" I said, using his new nickname. "We can do this!"

Emboldened by our initial success, I decided to push my luck. I took a few steps back. Bonji remained seated, eyes fixed on the treat in my hand.

"Good boy!" I praised, taking another step.

And another.

Bonji's head started to swivel. He glanced at a jogger passing by, then at a group of kids playing fetch with a Labrador. His tail thumped a hesitant rhythm.

"Stay, Bonji," I pleaded, my voice gaining a touch of desperation. The treat dangled precariously in my fingers.

The world seemed to slow down. A squirrel scampered across the path, its bushy tail a twitching temptation. Bonji whined, his gaze flickering between the treat and the furry interloper.

Bonji's Monologue:

(Inner monologue, full of puppy confusion)

"Squirrel! Treat! Squirrel! Treat! Which one? Oh boy, they're both so tempting! But Sarah said stay... maybe just a peek? No, bad Bonji! Focus! Treat... treat..."

My hand ached from holding the treat aloft. This obedience thing was harder than it looked!

(Back to narration):

Just as I thought he might break, Bonji surprised me. He let out a frustrated huff, then settled back down with a determined look. His eyes never left the treat.

Relief washed over me. "That's my boy!" I exclaimed, rushing back to him and showering him with praise. He lapped up the attention, his tongue lolling out in a goofy grin.

Perhaps, just perhaps, obedience wasn't a complete lost cause after all. Maybe, with patience and persistence, we could turn this ball of fluff into a well-mannered canine citizen.

As the afternoon sun cast long shadows across the park, I realized it wasn't just Bonji learning. I was learning too, about patience, communication, and the deep bond between a human and their dog. The road ahead might be filled with chewed furniture and muddy paw prints, but with each successful "sit" and focused glance, the joy and love in Bonji's golden eyes made it all worthwhile.

Chapter 18: The Silver Lining

- This chapter acknowledges the emotional toll of caring for a senior dog.
- Sarah might share a personal anecdote about a health scare with Bonji, emphasizing the importance of pet insurance and navigating the decision-making process with a veterinarian.
- The chapter could also delve into resources available for pet owners facing similar situations, like pet hospice care or support groups.

Chapter 18: The Big Splash

The morning sun cast long shadows across the park as Sarah tightened Bonji's leash. Today was the day they were finally tackling the dreaded "water obstacle" at dog training. Bonji, a golden retriever with a coat the color of sunshine, vibrated with excitement. Every rustle of leaves and chirp of a bird sent his tail wagging like a metronome set to "happy."

Sarah, however, wasn't quite as enthusiastic. Memories of Bonji's last bath – a symphony of splashing, barking, and escaping suds – sent shivers down her spine. Still, overcoming his fear of water was an important goal.

Reaching the training area, Sarah spotted the other dogs, all excitedly eyeing a small blue pool. Their owners stood nearby, offering encouragement – and treats. Bonji, ever the social butterfly, tried to greet them all at once, the leash tangling around Sarah's legs.

The trainer, a woman named Mary with a calm demeanor and endless patience, began the session. She first demonstrated the obstacle course, leading a fluffy poodle named Muffin through a series of tunnels and jumps before guiding her confidently across the pool. Muffin emerged dripping but proud, a triumphant bark escaping her tiny body.

Now it was Bonji's turn. Sarah held his leash loosely, offering him encouraging words and a handful of kibble. He inched closer, sniffing the edge of the pool with suspicion.

(Bonji's Monologue)

"Ugh, what is this? This smells… wet? And chlorine-y? It looks deep too. Maybe if I pretend not to see it, it'll go away? Or maybe I can dig a hole under it? Yeah, that sounds like a plan!"

Bonji started digging furiously at the grass beside the pool, sending Sarah scrambling to redirect him. Mary approached, her smile radiating warmth.

"Don't worry," she said, offering a reassuring pat to Bonji's head. "He's just being cautious. Let's try a little positive reinforcement."

Mary grabbed a squeaky toy, the kind that looked suspiciously like a giant chew toy in Bonji's eyes. She tossed it into the shallow end of the pool, sending a small wave crashing towards the bank.

Bonji's ears perked up. The forbidden zone suddenly held the key to his beloved squeaky friend! He glanced at Sarah, then back at the pool. A silent battle raged behind his golden eyes – fear versus squeaky toy.

The toy bobbed invitingly on the water's surface. Sarah, sensing a shift in Bonji's focus, crouched down and whispered, "Go get it, boy!"

Hesitantly, one paw dipped into the water. It was refreshingly cool, not scalding hot as Bonji had imagined. With a determined look, he took another step, the water lapping at his belly.

He finally reached the toy, the squeak escaping its rubber mouth in a high-pitched cry. But how to retrieve it? Jumping in seemed terrifying!

Suddenly, inspiration struck. Bonji crouched, extending his long neck and gently snatching the toy with his teeth. He retreated backwards, dragging the prize triumphantly back to dry land.

The world erupted in cheers. Sarah showered Bonji with praise and a shower of kibble. His tail wagged so hard his entire body wiggled. He had conquered the water obstacle!

Exhilarated, Bonji circled the pool, barking excitedly. Every so often, he'd glance back at Sarah with a proud grin, his fur glistening in the morning sun. He had faced his fear, and with a little encouragement, emerged a champion.

From that day forward, water wasn't the enemy anymore. It held the promise of splashing fun and squeaky toy victories. And Sarah, watching her golden retriever romp through the pool, couldn't help but smile. Maybe bath time wouldn't be quite so bad after all.

Life with a Golden (Chapters 19-23): This section expands the narrative beyond just Bonji. Sarah interviews other Golden Retriever owners, showcasing the unique personalities and quirks of the breed. Readers learn about Goldens as therapy dogs, service animals, and simply beloved family members.

Chapter 19: A Tapestry of Golden Personalities

- **Expanding the Focus:** This chapter shifts from Sarah and Bonji's story to explore the broader world of Golden Retrievers.
- **Golden Owners Unite:** Sarah interviews other Golden Retriever owners from various walks of life. This could include:
  - A family with a Golden Retriever as a therapy dog for their child with autism.
  - A single man whose Golden provides companionship and motivation for daily walks.
  - A couple who train their Golden Retriever as a service animal for a veteran with PTSD.
- **Breed Spotlight:** Each interview highlights the unique personalities and quirks that make Golden Retrievers so beloved.
  - Include anecdotes about their individual talents, funny habits, or specific ways they bring joy to their owners.

Chapter 19: Tails of Golden Love

The sun dripped golden honey across the park, casting long shadows as Sarah and Bonji strolled along the gravel path. Bonji, a magnificent Golden Retriever in the prime of his life, sniffed excitedly at every rustle in the bushes. Sarah, her heart overflowing with love, chuckled at his boundless curiosity.

"You're such a goofball, Bonji," she said, scratching him behind the ears. He thumped his tail against the ground, sending a flurry of leaves scattering in the breeze.

They reached a clearing where a group of people had gathered with their dogs. Sarah recognized them - it was the Golden Retriever meetup group she'd joined a few months ago. A wave of warmth washed over her. Here, surrounded by these beautiful, friendly dogs and their loving owners, she felt a sense of belonging.

"Bonji!" A familiar bark pierced the air. A ginger blur shot towards them, a ball of golden fur bouncing excitedly at its heels. It was Max, a rambunctious young Golden Retriever, Bonji's best friend at the park.

The two dogs launched into a joyous dance of play, chasing each other around the clearing, their barks echoing through the trees. Sarah watched them, a smile tugging at her lips.

"They're inseparable, aren't they?" A woman with salt-and-pepper hair approached Sarah, her own Golden Retriever, a gentle giant named Luna, trotting beside her.

"They are," Sarah agreed. "Max keeps Bonji young at heart."

Luna, all grace and poise, sniffed politely at Bonji before settling down beside him. Sarah and the woman, whose name was Emily, began to chat.

(Bonji's Monologue)

"Sniff, sniff...Luna! Hi there, beautiful! You smell like sunshine and belly rubs. Let's play chase with Max again! Wait, who's this human talking to Sarah? New friend? Gotta sniff and say hello!"

(End Monologue)

Bonji, ever the social butterfly, bounded over to Emily, showering her with enthusiastic doggy kisses. She laughed, patting his head.

As the conversation flowed, Sarah learned that Emily had adopted Luna as a therapy dog to help her cope with anxiety. Luna's calming presence and unconditional love had made a world of difference in Emily's life.

Sarah shared her own story about how Bonji had brought joy and companionship into her life. They talked about the challenges of training, the joys of long walks, and the quirky personalities that made Golden Retrievers so special.

As the afternoon wore on, other Golden Retrievers and their owners joined the group. Sarah witnessed a young girl struggling to control her exuberant puppy. A kind, older gentleman with a wise-looking Golden Retriever offered her some gentle training tips, guiding her with patience and understanding.

(Sarah's Reflection)

These dogs, with their soulful eyes and boundless energy, had a way of bringing people together. Here, amidst the laughter, barks, and wagging tails, differences faded away. There was a shared love for this remarkable breed, a bond forged by the unconditional love Golden Retrievers offer.

(End Reflection)

Watching the group of people and their dogs interact, Sarah felt a surge of gratitude. Bonji wasn't just her dog; he was a bridge, connecting her to a community of like-minded people who understood the magic of Golden Retrievers. The sun began its descent, painting the sky with hues of orange and pink. As it was time to leave, Sarah looked at Bonji, his tongue lolling out in a happy grin.

"Ready to go home, buddy?" she asked, her voice thick with emotion.

Bonji barked excitedly, then nudged his head against her hand. In that simple gesture, Sarah found all the confirmation she needed. Bonji brought joy into her life, but through him, she had also found friendship, support, and a deeper appreciation for the extraordinary bond between humans and Golden Retrievers.

Chapter 20: Golden at Work

- **Beyond the Family Unit:** This chapter explores the diverse roles Golden Retrievers play beyond being pets.
- **Canine Careers:**
  - Feature a profile of a Golden Retriever working as a guide dog for the visually impaired.
  - Highlight the training process and the incredible bond between these dogs and their handlers.
  - Briefly touch on other working Golden Retrievers in fields like search and rescue or detection work.
- **Therapy and Assistance:**
  - Discuss the emotional support Golden Retrievers provide in therapeutic settings.
  - Share stories of their impact on children in hospitals or individuals struggling with anxiety or depression.

Chapter 20: The Whisper of Change

The crisp autumn air swirled fallen leaves around Sarah's ankles as she walked Bonji through the park. The golden leaves mirrored the hue of Bonji's fur, once vibrant and full, now tinged with a hint of silver at the muzzle. His gait was slower, his playful leaps replaced by a measured trot.

A pang of sadness squeezed Sarah's heart. Denial had been a comforting blanket for a while, but the truth was undeniable – Bonji was aging.

They reached their usual spot, a large oak tree that had witnessed countless games of fetch and lazy afternoons spent napping in the dappled sunlight. Sarah sank onto the familiar bench, Bonji settling beside her with a contented sigh.

(Sarah's Monologue)

"Remember when you were a whirlwind of fur and energy, Bonji? You'd chase squirrels with reckless abandon, turning this whole park into your personal obstacle course. You'd chew through every shoe you could find, and those puppy-dog eyes could melt anyone's heart, even when you were up to no good."

A small smile tugged at Sarah's lips as warm memories flooded her mind.

"We've come a long way, haven't we boy? You learned to fetch without destroying everything in your path, mastered the art of 'stay,' and became the best cuddler a girl could ask for. You were my rock, my constant companion through thick and thin."

Sarah reached down, gently stroking Bonji's fur. His soft whines were a familiar comfort, a constant reminder of the bond they shared.

"Now, things are slowing down. Those endless sprints have turned into leisurely walks, and you spend more time napping than chasing butterflies. But you know what, Bonji? That's okay."

A tear escaped, tracing a warm path down her cheek.

"We can't outrun time, can we boy? But even as your golden years slow you down, your love shines just as bright. Maybe even brighter, because it feels more precious somehow, knowing it won't last forever."

Sarah pulled Bonji close, burying her face in his fur. The familiar scent of dog and sunshine brought a wave of bittersweet comfort.

"Every walk, every cuddle, every shared sunrise – it all means more now, Bonji. We'll savor every moment, because you're not just a dog, you're my family. And even though this chapter is ending, our story isn't over yet. We'll face whatever comes together, just like we always have."

With a shaky breath, Sarah lifted her head, gazing out at the park bathed in the golden glow of the afternoon sun. There was a new awareness in her eyes, a quiet acceptance of the inevitable changes. But amidst the bitter-sweetness, there was also a fierce love, a determination to cherish every remaining moment with her golden companion.

Chapter 21: Adventures with your Golden

- **Golden Getaways:** This chapter focuses on the active lifestyle Golden Retrievers enjoy and how owners can include them in adventures.
- **Planning Dog-Friendly Trips:**
    - Offer tips on finding dog-friendly accommodations, restaurants with outdoor seating, and activities suitable for both humans and canine companions.
    - Include personal anecdotes about Sarah and Mike taking Bonji on hikes, dog park visits, or even dog-friendly vacations.
- **Golden Games:**
    - Provide a list of fun and engaging activities to keep Golden Retrievers mentally and physically stimulated, like fetch, agility training, or swimming (if your dog enjoys it).

Chapter 21: The Unseen World

The crisp autumn air nipped at Sarah's cheeks as she walked Bonji through the park. Leaves, once vibrant greens and fiery oranges, now swirled in a kaleidoscope of browns at their feet. Bonji, ever the playful pup, snatched at a rogue leaf, sending it fluttering into the air before chasing after it with a joyous bark.

Sarah couldn't help but smile. Time seemed to melt away as she watched him, his golden fur catching the dappled sunlight filtering through the trees. Bonji had been by her side for five years now, and it felt like just yesterday she was fumbling with a leash and trying to decipher his puppy yaps.

Lately, though, a subtle shift had settled over Bonji. His once boundless energy seemed a little subdued. He'd spend more time curled up by her feet, his gaze fixed on seemingly nothing at all.

Reaching the park bench, Sarah sank down, Bonji panting happily beside her. Gazing out at the expanse of the park, a monologue tumbled from her lips, a question she'd been wrestling with for weeks.

(Sarah's Monologue)

"Bonji, old boy," she began, her voice soft. "Do you ever wonder what's out there? Beyond the squirrels you chase and the treats I hide in the backyard? Do you sense things I can't? Sometimes, when you stare off into the distance, I swear you see something I don't."

She knelt, scratching behind his ears, her touch eliciting a contented sigh from the dog.

"Maybe it's birds I can't hear, or scents carried on the wind that I can't smell. Maybe there's a whole world you experience that's invisible to me."

A pang of sadness tugged at her heart. The thought of a world she couldn't share with her beloved companion was a bittersweet notion.

"But then I look at you, Bonji," she continued, her voice catching slightly. "Your tail wags, your eyes sparkle… and I know all I need to know. You're happy. You feel loved, safe, and secure. And that's all that truly matters."

She fell silent, the weight of her unspoken question settling between them.

As if in response, Bonji nudged her hand with his wet nose, his golden eyes conveying a depth of understanding that transcended words. Sarah smiled, a tear slipping down her cheek.

Perhaps the unseen world remained just that – unseen. But the bond between them, the love that flowed between human and dog, was a language they both understood perfectly.

The sun dipped lower in the sky, casting long shadows across the park. Sarah rose, brushing off fallen leaves. With one last glance at the vast expanse of the unseen, she looped the leash around Bonji's collar.

"Homeward bound, boy," she said, her voice filled with a newfound acceptance.

Bonji barked once, a happy sound that echoed through the crisp autumn air. Together, they walked into the setting sun, their silhouettes merging into a single image of unwavering companionship.

Chapter 22: Keeping Your Golden Golden

- **Senior Years:** This chapter delves into caring for a Golden Retriever in its golden years.
- **Adapting to Age:**
  - Discuss the importance of regular veterinary checkups for senior dogs.
  - Offer tips on adjusting exercise routines to accommodate aging joints, choosing senior-friendly food options, and recognizing signs of potential health issues.
- **Staying Active, Staying Happy:**
  - Emphasize the importance of maintaining a level of physical and mental activity appropriate for senior dogs.
  - Suggest low-impact exercises like gentle walks or swimming and engaging brain games designed for senior canines.

Chapter 22: The Golden Sunset

The crisp autumn air swirled fallen leaves around my feet as I walked Bonji along our usual path. The setting sun cast an orange glow on the park, painting long shadows from the trees. Bonji, once a ball of boundless energy, trotted beside me at a slower pace these days. His once bright golden fur was dusted with a touch of grey around his muzzle.

We stopped at our favorite bench, the one overlooking the small lake. Bonji lowered himself with a soft sigh, his once-powerful legs a little stiffer now. I sat beside him, stroking his head, the familiar warmth a comfort in the cooling evening.

"Remember this bench, Bonji?" I began, a soft smile gracing my lips. "This is where we used to sit after your puppy obedience class. You'd learned 'sit' and 'stay,' so proud of yourself, tail wagging like a metronome on overdrive."

A chuckle escaped my lips as I reminisced. "We spent countless hours here, Bonji. You chasing squirrels, me throwing your favorite squeaky ball until your tongue lolled out. You were a hurricane of golden fur back then, a ball of endless energy."

I paused, gazing at the fiery hues bleeding across the sky. "We've had some amazing adventures together, haven't we boy? Remember that time you learned to swim at the lake house? You were so scared at first, then you took off like a furry torpedo. We had to chase you around the entire lake that day!"

A bittersweet pang hit my chest. "Those were the days, weren't they? You were always up for anything, my golden shadow. Now..." My voice hitched slightly. "Now, our walks are a little slower, your games a little calmer. But you know what, Bonji?"

I looked down at him, his kind brown eyes reflecting the setting sun. "The love hasn't changed a bit. You may be slowing down, but the way you look at me with that goofy grin, the way you nudge your head for a scratch behind the ears – that love, Bonji, that's as strong as ever."

I wrapped my arm around him, the familiar weight a source of comfort. "We may be facing a golden sunset, old friend, but the memories we've made will forever paint our lives with warmth. And who knows, maybe someday down the road, there'll be another furry friend to share our adventures, another golden heart to fill this space beside me."

A tear escaped my eye, tracing a warm path down my cheek. I leaned down and kissed the top of Bonji's head. "Thank you, Bonji, for everything. You've been the best friend a person could ask for."

The sun dipped below the horizon, casting long shadows across the park. We sat in comfortable silence, Bonji resting his head on my lap, the gentle rise and fall of his breath a comforting rhythm. As twilight painted the sky, I knew that our journey together was nearing its end, but the love we shared, the memories we made, would forever shine brightly in the golden sunset of our time together.

Chapter 23: The Unconditional Bond: Facing Loss

- **A Delicate Topic:** This chapter acknowledges the inevitable - the possibility of losing a beloved pet.
- **Sharing Sarah's Experience (Optional):**
  - If Sarah has personally experienced the loss of a pet, she could share her story in a sensitive and relatable way.
  - Focus on the grieving process, honoring the memories, and the deep bond shared with a canine companion.
- **General Advice:**
  - Offer resources for pet loss support or guidance on making end-of-life decisions for pets.
  - Emphasize the importance of cherishing every moment with your Golden Retriever and creating lasting memories.

Chapter 23: A Walk Down Memory Lane

The crisp autumn air swirled fallen leaves around my ankles as I walked Bonji through the park. His gait wasn't as sprightly as it used to be, his once boundless energy replaced by a contented trot. But his golden fur still gleamed in the afternoon sun, and his tail thumped a steady rhythm against the ground.

We stopped by the bench where, ten years ago, a tiny ball of fluff with clumsy paws had first captured my heart. I remembered the sleepless nights, the chewed furniture, the endless puddles on the floor. But those fleeting moments of chaos were eclipsed by a lifetime of loyalty, laughter, and unconditional love.

(Inner Monologue)

Sitting here with Bonji, it's like watching a movie reel of our life together flash before my eyes.

I can still picture him as a puppy, his head barely reaching my knee, eyes wide with curiosity. He'd chase butterflies with a goofy grin, his floppy ears flapping in the wind. Obedience classes were a hilarious blur of tangled leashes, chewed treats, and Bonji's boundless enthusiasm for greeting every single person he met.

(Inner Monologue)

There were chewed shoes, yes, and furniture redecorated in drool. But there were also those first tentative steps off the leash, the proud moment he mastered "sit," and the countless walks that filled our days with sunshine and laughter.

Bonji nudged my hand, his eyes reflecting the same golden light of the setting sun. We'd explored countless miles of trails together, his wet nose leading the way through fields and forests. He'd been my constant companion through thick and thin, a silent confidante and furry therapist.

(Inner Monologue)

There were tough days, too. Days when work stressed me out, or relationships crumbled. But Bonji was always there, a warm, furry presence at my feet, reminding me of the simple joys in life.

He let out a soft whine, his head tilting in concern. I knelt down, burying my face in his thick fur. "It's okay, boy," I whispered. "We'll get through this, just like we always have." He licked my cheek with a sandpapery tongue, a silent promise of unwavering devotion.

(Inner Monologue)

I know these golden years won't last forever. But the memories we've made, the love we've shared, that's something no time can take away. You're more than just a pet, Bonji. You're family.

Squeezing his leash, I stood up. The park was emptying, and the first chill of twilight settled in the air. We walked home, my heart full of a bittersweet gratitude. Bonji may be slowing down, but the love that shone in his eyes remained as bright as ever. And as long as I had him by my side, our golden journey would continue, one cherished memory at a time.

Unexpected Challenges (Chapters 24-25): The book acknowledges the inevitable - the challenges of caring for a dog through illness. Sarah shares her experience (or creates a fictional scenario) of dealing with a health issue with Bonji, emphasizing the importance of pet insurance, senior dog care, and the emotional toll of pet loss.

Chapter 24: The Golden Years Slow Down

The morning sun filtered through the blinds, painting golden stripes across the living room floor. I stretched, the familiar creak of my knees a new, unwelcome sound. Yawning, I padded over to the bed, expecting to find Bonji, my golden retriever, sprawled at the foot.

He wasn't there.

A frown creased my forehead. Usually, he'd greet me with a flurry of excited barks and a wet nose nudging my hand. "Bonji?" I called out, my voice tinged with worry.

He emerged from the hallway, his gait slower, his tail held lower than usual. The spring had gone out of his step, replaced by a cautious shuffle. My heart ached. He was getting old.

He thumped his tail a few times against the floor, a tired greeting that filled me with a pang of nostalgia. I knelt down, my hand instinctively reaching for his head. His fur felt a little duller, not as soft and plush as it used to be. He leaned into my touch, his golden eyes holding a familiar warmth, yet a hint of something else – a flicker of confusion, perhaps?

"Hey, good boy," I murmured, scratching behind his ears. He didn't respond with his usual enthusiastic wiggle. Instead, he let out a soft sigh, a sound that resonated with a strange familiarity. It was the sigh of getting older, of a body that wasn't quite as young and energetic as it once was.

A lump formed in my throat. We'd been through so much together, Bonji and I. He'd been by my side through thick and thin, my constant companion, my furry confidante. He'd seen me at my best and my worst, offering unconditional love and a wagging tail no matter what. Now, it was my turn to be there for him, to support him as he entered this new chapter of his life.

Inner Monologue:

These past few weeks, I've noticed the little changes. He doesn't seem as interested in his frisbee anymore. Our walks are shorter, his pace slower. Maybe it's just me imagining things, but sometimes, when he looks at me, there's a question in his eyes. A question I can't quite answer. How much longer do we have together? The thought itself is unbearable. But I have to be strong, for him. We'll adjust our routines, find new ways to spend our days. Maybe shorter walks in the park, more cuddle time on the couch. I'll make sure his golden years are filled with love, comfort, and all the belly rubs he can handle.

With a determined smile, I scooped up his favorite plush bone and tossed it a short distance across the room. He watched it land with a disinterested gaze, then let out a weak purr. It wasn't the enthusiastic chase I was used to, but it was enough. It was a sign that a part of that playful spirit still flickered within him.

"Maybe not frisbee today, huh boy?" I said, kneeling back down. "How about a nice belly rub instead?"

His tail thumped a little faster as I scratched his furry belly. He closed his eyes, a content sigh escaping his lips. In that moment, the world seemed to melt away. There was just me, him, and the quiet comfort of our bond. A bond that transcended age, a love that wouldn't diminish with time. We would face this new chapter together, side by side, my golden retriever and me.

Chapter 25: Facing the Inevitable

- This chapter deals with the emotional and practical aspects of caring for a Golden Retriever facing illness.
- It could be based on Sarah's real experience or a fictional scenario where Bonji develops a health issue.
- The narrative can explore:
    - The emotional toll of seeing your beloved dog unwell.
    - The importance of pet insurance in covering medical costs.
    - Making difficult decisions about treatment options.
    - Highlighting the value of veterinary support and palliative care.
- The chapter can end on a bittersweet note, acknowledging the challenges but emphasizing the importance of making your dog's remaining time as comfortable and loving as possible.

Chapter 25: Forever in My Heart

The past few weeks had been a blur. Bonji, my golden sunshine, my furry shadow, seemed to shrink a little each day. His once boundless energy had dwindled to quiet naps by the window. Walks, once a joyous exploration of every sniff-worthy corner, were now slow, deliberate strolls.

The vet's confirmation echoed in my ears: age-related ailments. We were navigating a path neither of us wanted to be on, a path paved with love, worry, and the gut-wrenching reality of time's relentless march.

This morning, Bonji didn't greet me with his usual enthusiastic tail wags. He lay on his favorite rug, eyes cloudy with a film I hadn't noticed before. My heart ached. I knelt beside him, stroking his soft fur, the familiar warmth a comfort against the growing chill of fear.

"Hey, champ," I whispered, my voice thick with unshed tears. "How are you feeling today?"

His gaze met mine, a spark of recognition flickering within. A weak wag of his tail, a faint attempt at a smile. It was all I needed.

"It's okay, Bonji," I continued, my voice catching. "We're in this together. You've always been by my side, and I won't leave yours now."

Memories flooded in: puppyhood's chaotic joy, countless walks filled with playful nips at dandelions, evenings curled up on the couch, his head resting contentedly on my lap. A lifetime of companionship condensed into a montage of pure love.

"Remember our first walk in the park? You chased every squirrel with the fervor of a tiny golden knight," I chuckled, a watery smile tracing my lips.

His head tilted slightly, a flicker of recognition in his cloudy eyes. He let out a soft whine, a sound that ripped through my heart.

"You were the best dog anyone could ask for, Bonji," I confessed, tears finally spilling over. "Loyal, loving, always happy to see me. You brought so much sunshine into my life."

I reached for a chew toy, the one he'd loved the most as a puppy. He lifted his head with a valiant effort, but it dropped again.

"It's okay, boy," I murmured, taking the toy and placing it beside him. "Rest now. You've earned it."

Silence settled between us, a heavy quiet punctuated only by his shallow breaths. I pulled out his favorite blanket, wrapping it around his trembling form. It was a small gesture, offering comfort in the face of the inevitable.

"I love you, Bonji," I whispered, burying my face in his fur, inhaling the familiar scent of dog and sunshine. "Always."

He didn't respond, but a single tear trickled down my cheek and landed on his fur. In that moment, I knew. Our journey together was nearing its end, but the love we shared would forever be etched in my heart.

Epilogue: A Golden Legacy

- The epilogue offers a sense of closure and hope.
- Sarah reflects on the journey with Bonji, the lessons learned, and the unconditional love these dogs bring.
- It could feature:
    - Heartfelt memories of Bonji's life.
    - Photos showcasing special moments.
    - A message about the importance of cherishing each day with your furry companion.

Optional Ending:

- The epilogue could leave the door open for a new chapter. Sarah and Mike might consider adopting another Golden Retriever puppy, highlighting the enduring bond humans share with this special breed.

A soft whimper escapes his lips, and I pull him closer. In that moment, all the world fades away, leaving only the warmth of his fur, the gentle rhythm of his breath, and the unbreakable bond that transcends words.

He may be leaving, but the love he leaves behind will forever be a part of me. And perhaps, someday down the road, when my heart is ready, another golden light will fill this space, carrying forward the legacy of love, laughter, and loyalty that began with a puppy named Bonji.